C000172222

Crazy Jack

Brandon Robshaw

Published in association with
The Basic Skills Agency

Hodder & Stoughton
A MEMBER OF THE HODDER HEADLINE GROUP

Acknowledgements
Cover: Dave Smith
Illustrations: Dave Hopkins

Orders: please contact Bookpoint Ltd, 78 Milton Park, Abingdon, Oxon OX14
4TD. Telephone: (44) 01235 827720, Fax: (44) 01235 400454. Lines are open
from 9.00–6.00, Monday to Saturday, with a 24-hour message answering service.
Email address: orders@bookpoint.co.uk

British Library Cataloguing in Publication Data
A catalogue record for this title is available from The British Library

ISBN 0 340 80054 2

First published 2001
Impression number   10 9 8 7 6 5 4 3 2 1
Year   2007 2006 2005 2004 2003 2002 2001

Copyright © 2001 Brandon Robshaw

Typeset by SX Composing DTP, Rayleigh, Essex.
Printed in Great Britain for Hodder & Stoughton Educational, a division of
Hodder Headline Plc, 338 Euston Road, London NW1 3BH
by Athenæum Press Ltd, Gateshead, Tyne & Wear.

Crazy Jack

Contents

1

Crazy Jack

Simon found Crazy Jack
at a car boot sale.
Crazy Jack was a dummy.
A painted wooden dummy,
about a metre high.
He had red hair,
a freckled face,
and a cheeky grin.

Simon picked him up.
'Hey, I like this dummy.
What do you think, Kirstie?'
Kirstie was Simon's wife.

'I don't like it,' said Kirstie.
'I don't like its face.'

The dummy turned to look at Kirstie.
'Look who's talking!' it said
in a squeaky little voice.
'Take a look in the mirror sometime!'

Kirstie was shocked for a moment.
Then she looked at Simon.
'Simon, that was you wasn't it?'

Simon laughed.
'Yes – there's a knob at the back
that makes its mouth open and shut.
I'm good at doing the voice, aren't I?
I could use it in my act.'

'Don't,' said Kirstie.
'I don't like it. Just leave it.'

'No, I think it's really good,' said Simon.
He turned to the man behind the stall.
'How much?'

'Twenty quid,' said the man.

'I'll take it,' said Simon.
He walked away with the dummy on his arm.
'What shall I call you?' he asked.

The dummy's mouth opened.
'Crazy Jack,' it squeaked.

'Right!' said Simon. 'Crazy Jack it is.
Isn't that weird, Kirstie?
That name just came to me.
What do you think?'

'I think you've wasted twenty quid,'
said Kirstie.

2

A Hard Life

Simon was a stand-up comedian.
Not a famous one.
He wasn't on television.
He made his living by working the
holiday camps in seaside towns.

Kirstie worked the holiday camps too.
She was a singer.
That was how they'd met.

Between them, they just about
made a living.
In the winter,
there was no work.
They had to try to save money in the summer
to get through the year.

It was a hard life.
Playing in half-empty halls
at the end of the season.
Playing to audiences
who talked all the way through the act.

Sometimes, Simon felt sick of it.
He had once dreamed of being a star.
But that didn't look like happening.
No, he'd never be a star.
Just a second-rate comedian
playing third-rate holiday camps.
It was hard not to lose heart.

Until Crazy Jack came along.
Then everything changed.

3

Staying Up Late

Simon practised all evening.
He sat with Crazy Jack on his knee,
talking with him.
He found it easy to work Crazy Jack.
He could make the eyes and the mouth move
so naturally, the dummy looked alive.
He did a cheeky, squeaky voice
which sounded just right for Crazy Jack.
He was very good at talking
without moving his lips.

He never had to try and think
what Crazy Jack should say.
The words just came out –
as if the dummy itself was talking.

Kirstie hated it.
'Come on, Simon. It's time for bed.
Stop talking to that horrible dummy.'

Simon yawned. 'All right
I'd better put you in your box, Crazy Jack.'

'No, don't put me in the box!'
squeaked Crazy Jack.
'It's not time for bed yet.
We need to practise more.'

'All right, just a bit longer,' said Simon.

'Well, I'm going to bed,' said Kirstie.

'Go on then,' squeaked Crazy Jack.
'Best place for you!'

'What?' said Kirstie.

'I said goodnight,' squeaked Crazy Jack.
'Sleep tight. Hope the bugs don't bite!'

Kirstie went into the bedroom.
She slammed the door.
She tried to sleep.
She could hear Crazy Jack's squeaky voice
coming through the wall.
It seemed to go on all night.

4

Crazy Jack's First Gig

When Kirstie woke up next morning,
Simon wasn't in the bed.
She went downstairs.

He was still sitting in the armchair
with Crazy Jack on his knee.
He looked tired.

'Have you been here all night?' asked Kirstie.
'You look terrible!'

'Look who's talking!' squeaked Crazy Jack.
'If I had a face like yours, I'd get a transplant!'

'Shut up, Simon,' said Kirstie.

'What?' said Simon.
'I didn't say anything – it was Crazy Jack!'

'That's not funny,' said Kirstie.

That night, Simon used Crazy Jack in his act.
The act was a great success.
Crazy Jack had the audience in stitches.
Most of them, anyway.
He picked on a few people –
a fat woman and a man with a bald head –
and made fun of them.

Simon was surprised at himself.
It was as if all his nasty, cruel side
came out in Crazy Jack.
It wasn't much fun if you were picked on.
But the rest of the audience loved it.

After the show, the manager booked Simon
for the rest of the summer.

'What do you think, Kirstie?'
asked Simon after the show.
'It went down well, didn't it?'

'Yes,' said Kirstie. 'But I didn't like it.
You were too cruel to those poor people.'

'It wasn't him,' squeaked Crazy Jack.
'It was me!'

5

Success!

Simon earned good money.
The manager gave Simon and Kirstie
a caravan to stay in on the camp site.

'Isn't it great not to worry about paying
the rent any more?' said Simon.

'I suppose so,' said Kirstie.
'But I wish it wasn't thanks to that horrible
doll. I hate it. It's so cruel to people.'

'It's just an act, Kirstie,' said Simon.

'But she hasn't got the brain to see that,'
squeaked Crazy Jack.
'She's got a brain the size of a pea!'

'Stop it!' said Kirstie. 'I hate that doll.
I'd like to smash it. Smash it to pieces!'

Crazy Jack turned his head.
His eyes rolled towards Kirstie.
'If anyone gets smashed,' he squeaked,
'it won't be me – it'll be you!'

'Don't, Simon,' said Kirstie.
'You're scaring me.
Please – put the doll down.'

Simon put Crazy Jack down.
'Sorry,' he said.
'Sometimes Crazy Jack just says these things.
I can't stop him.
It doesn't mean anything.'

'Please, Simon – get rid of him.'

Simon shook his head. 'I can't.
There's a big talent contest coming up.
A TV producer is going to be there.
If I win, we've got it made.
And I'm bound to win with Crazy Jack!'

6

Marvin Flame

Simon had only one real rival
in the talent contest.
The rival was a singer called Marvin Flame.
Simon had seen his act.
He had to admit it was good.

He felt a bit fed up when he found out Marvin
was going in for the talent contest.
'I wish he wasn't going in for it,'
he said to Kirstie.

'I know,' said Kirstie.
'He's good. A class act.'

'He's rubbish!' squeaked Crazy Jack.
'We'll beat him, won't we, Simon?'

'I hope so,' said Simon.

'We'll have to practise,'
squeaked Crazy Jack.
'And make the act better and better!'

So, night after night,
after Kirstie had gone to bed,
they sat up practising.
Simon often felt tired.
He wanted to go to bed,
but Crazy Jack wouldn't let him.

'We've got to practise,' he squeaked.
'We've got to beat Marvin Flame.'

'I wish he wasn't going in for it,'
said Simon.

'Do you?' squeaked Crazy Jack.
'Then maybe we should stop him!'

There was a silence.
'What do you mean?' asked Simon.

'He could have a little accident,'
squeaked Crazy Jack.
'Do you know what I mean?'

Simon stared at Crazy Jack.
Crazy Jack grinned at him.
'Leave it to me!' squeaked Crazy Jack.
'I'll think of something.'

Simon didn't say anything.
He felt a chill run through him.

7

Fire!

'I've got a plan!' squeaked Crazy Jack
the next night.
Kirstie was in bed.
Simon wanted to go to bed too but
Crazy Jack had made him stay up to practise.

'What do you mean, a plan?'

'A plan to get rid of Marvin Flame,'
squeaked Crazy Jack.

'I don't want to hear it,' said Simon.

'You're soft, Simon. A great big softy!
Listen to me. Here's the plan.
Marvin Flame is going to go up in flames!'

'No,' said Simon. 'Forget it.'

'Come on, Simon,' squeaked Crazy Jack.
'I need you to help me.'

'No,' said Simon. 'I don't want to.'

Crazy Jack grinned at him.
'That's too bad –
because you're coming with me!'

Simon got up.
He didn't want to,
but he couldn't help it.
He opened the door of the caravan.
He stepped out into the cool night air.
Crazy Jack was in his arms.

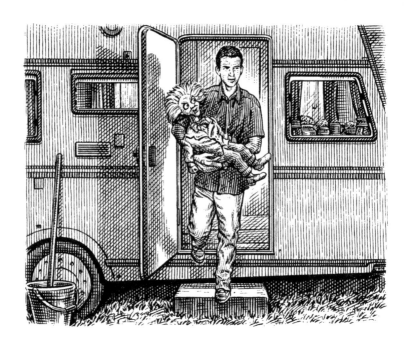

'This way, Simon,' squeaked Crazy Jack.
'To the garage. We need a tin of petrol.'

'Please – I don't want to do this,' said Simon.

'You know you do really,' squeaked Crazy Jack.
They went to the garage.
They found a tin of petrol.

'Now to Marvin Flame's caravan,'
squeaked Crazy Jack. 'It's this way.'

'We shouldn't do this,' said Simon.
But he found himself walking
to Marvin's caravan.

'Here we are,' squeaked Crazy Jack.
'Sprinkle the petrol on it.'
Simon sprinkled the petrol on.

'Lovely!
Got a match?'

Simon took out a box of matches.

'You know what to do,' squeaked Crazy Jack.

'No – I can't . . .'

'Do it,' squeaked Crazy Jack.

With trembling fingers. Simon struck a match.
He threw it at Marvin Flame's caravan.
He jumped back.

A sheet of orange flame shot up
into the dark sky.

8

Owning Up

Marvin Flame didn't die.
He woke up just in time.
He got out of the caravan,
but he was badly hurt.
He burned his hands getting out
and he breathed in a lot of smoke.
It burned his throat.
He wouldn't be singing for a long time.
If ever again.

No one knew who had started the fire.
The manager of the holiday camp
started a collection for Marvin.
Simon put in fifty pounds.

'That was good of you,' said Kirstie.
'But in a way, it's lucky for you, isn't it?
Poor Marvin won't be going in
for the talent contest now.'

'It has nothing to do with luck,'
squeaked Crazy Jack.
'We sorted it, didn't we, Simon?'

'Shut up!' said Simon.

'What?' said Kirstie.
She looked at Crazy Jack's grinning face.
'What did you say?'

'We sorted it!' squeaked Crazy Jack.
'Me and Simon.
I was the brains –
but Simon lit the match!'

Kirstie looked at Simon.
'Tell me you're joking,' she said.
'Tell me this isn't true.
You could have killed him!
Have you gone out of your mind?'

'It wasn't my fault,' said Simon.
'It was Crazy Jack's idea.
He made me do it!'

'You're the crazy one,' said Kirstie.
'That horrible doll has driven you mad.
You've got to get rid of it, Simon!'

'He'll never get rid of me!'
squeaked Crazy Jack.

'I – I'd like to,' said Simon.
'But – I'm scared.
I don't dare.'

'Well, I dare!' said Kirstie.
She jumped up, snatched Crazy Jack
and ran out into the night.

9

Goodbye, Crazy Jack!

Kirstie ran through the caravan site and
down the road to the cliff path.
She stood at the top of the cliff.
Below, the sea crashed against the rocks.
'Goodbye, Crazy Jack!' shouted Kirstie.

She lifted him up high.
His head rolled round and stared at her.
Then something impossible happened.
Crazy Jack spoke.

'If I'm going down,
you're coming with me,' he squeaked.

Kirstie lost her balance.
She slipped and fell,
with Crazy Jack in her arms.
Down, down, down they fell,
onto the rocks below.

The coastguard broke the news to Simon.
Kirstie was dead.
Her body was found on the rocks.
They'd found Crazy Jack
floating in the water nearby.
The coastguard brought him back to Simon.

Simon sat in his caravan for a long time,
not speaking, staring at Crazy Jack.

At last, he picked him up.
'What happened?' he said.

'Don't worry about it, Simon,'
squeaked Crazy Jack.
'You're better off without her.
It'll be better, just the two of us.'

Simon didn't say anything.

'Come on, Simon,' squeaked Crazy Jack.
'Cheer up.
It's the talent contest next week.
We need to practise.'